Greater Than a Tourist - The Hague Zuid-Holland Netherlands

50 Travel Tips from a Local

Bárbara Campos Diniz

Lock Haven, PA

All rights reserved.

ISBN: 9781521825167

>TOURIST

Bárbara Campos Diniz

BOOK DESCRIPTION

Are you excited about planning your next trip?

Do you want to try something new while traveling?

Would you like some guidance from a local?

If you answered yes to any of these questions, then this book is just for you.

Greater Than a Tourist by Bárbara Campos Diniz offers the inside scope on The Hague, Netherlands. Most travel books tell you how to travel like a tourist. Although there's nothing wrong with that, as a part of the Greater than a Tourist series, this book will give you travel tips from someone who lives at your next travel destination.

In these pages you'll discover local advice that will help you throughout your stay. This book will not tell you exact addresses or store hours but instead will give you an excitement and knowledge from a local that you may not find in other smaller print travel books. Travel like a local. Slow down, stay in one place, and get to know the people and the culture of a place.

By the time you finish this book, you will be eager and prepared to travel to your next destination.

Bárbara Campos Diniz

TABLE OF CONTENTS

19. Enjoy the International Fireworks Festival

20. Eat as Much as You Can in the Hague Food Festival

21. Visit the Museum van Kleef

23. Look up, Never Down

24. Take a Walk Through China Town

25. Relax at the Grote Markt

26. De Pip is the Place to Be

27. Take a Look at the Peace Palace

28. See the Sint Jacobskerk

29. Go See a Musical

30. Discover the Paard van Troje

31. We'll Never Be Royals

32. Let's Party!

33. Be Godzilla for One Day

34. Contemplate the Binnenhof

35. Take a Look at the Ridderzaal

36. A Walk Through the Japanese Garden

37. Visit the Rose Garden

38. Go to the Museum Gevangenpoort

39. Mauritshuis, a Must See

40. Visit the Hague Municipal Museum

41. The Escher in het Paleis

42. Shop Till You Drop

43. Finding Vintage Shops

44. Hiking in the Meijendel Park

45. Having a Great Day in Scheveningen

DEDICATION

This book is dedicated to every student and young adult living studying in the Hague. Without you, I wouldn't have had fun in this marvelous city.

Bárbara Campos Diniz

ABOUT THE AUTHOR

Bárbara Campos Diniz is an exchange student who lived in the Hague for the past six months. She loves reading and writing and thought that by making this book with all the tips of the places she visited, she would be forever have a fun record of her adventures. She's travelled a lot in Europe and in the Netherlands and is proud to call the Dutch city her second home. There are a lot of hacks that she found out on her own and some that she found out through her Dutch friends and colleagues.

Bárbara Campos Diniz

HOW TO USE THIS BOOK

This book was written by someone who has lived in an area for over three months. The author has made the best suggestions based on their own experiences in the area. Please check that these places are still available before traveling to the area. The goal of this book is to help travelers either dream or experience different locations by providing opinions from a local.

Bárbara Campos Diniz

FROM THE PUBLISHER

Traveling can be one of the most important moments in a person's life. The memories that you have of anticipating going somewhere new or getting to travel are some of the best. As a publisher of the Greater Than a Tourist book series, as well as the popular 50 Things to Know book series, we strive to help you learn about new places, spark your imagination, and inspire you.

Thought this book you will find something for every traveler. Wherever you are and whatever you do I wish you safe fun, and inspiring travel.

Lisa Rusczyk Ed. D.
CZYK Publishing

Bárbara Campos Diniz

WELCOME TO > TOURIST

Bárbara Campos Diniz

INTRODUCTION

The Hague is a world city with a beautiful beach and an amazing sea. Due to the multiple courts present and historically grown political center, the offers many possibilities to let (international) law prevail. The historic and modern architecture is settled in a green environment, where people can learn, sport and relax. Together with the diverse population, the royal traditions are kept alive and being modernized. The multicultural background of the inhabitants offers the perfect environment for locals and tourists to interact in a friendly manner. The city helps people to be and to feel free. The extensive coast line is the place to be if you want to clear your mind after a business meeting. The coast line offers water sports, relaxation, high quality hospitality businesses, and walking or cycling through the dunes.

Bárbara Campos Diniz

1. Finding Your Way Around the City: VVV

Every city in the Netherlands has an office of the *Vereninging vood Vreemdelingenverkeer*, or VVV for short, near the municipality. In the Hague the VVV is located right in the city center and near the Central Station, making it accessible for all everyone in need. The VVV is the Dutch tourism organization that was designed not only to help tourists with directions, but to promote events, festivals and expositions in the city.

In the Hague, the VVV helps tourists around the city, suggests museums and galleries to be visited, restaurants, bike tours, the current plays in the theatre, they basically have all information of what's going on around the city. Their services are basically personalized once you start to talk to an attendant and explain what you're looking for in your experience in the Hague. All the times I visited the VVV I didn't need to try to speak Dutch because all of the attendants speak English and I got all my questions answered in a polite and more than satisfactory way.

2. Saving Money in Transportation

The transportation system in the Hague is amazing. There are trams, busses and subways to and from every part of the city, making it really easy to explore all the Hague has to offer. When I got here, the first thing I did was to buy an OV-Chipkaart in the train station. Everyone can do the same, it doesn't matter if you're Dutch or not.

The OV is the cheapest way to travel in all kinds of transportation in the Netherlands. It allows the cardholder to take a train, then a bus and a tram if necessary. The card also allows the cardholder to pay less within the city transportation. This means that in my case, for example, I pay the route I take from point A to point B rather than paying one full ticket. I saved a lot of money with my card and I don't get out of my house without it anymore.

3. The Apps That Will Make Your Life Easier

There are two basic apps that everyone in the Netherlands has installed in their phones and they also have to do with transportation. The NS App and the 9292 App. Both of them are available for Apple and Android users, are free, and they have saved me more times that I care to admit.

NS is the Dutch train company and this amazing app not only shows the number of existing routes there are from one place to the other, but   it also shows the fares of both first and second class and provides live information to the user regarding the changes of time, platform and a live GPS tracker that allows passengers to see where they are in the route and which station they are nearing.

The 9292 App works nationwide and also shows the number of routes there are from one place to the other and the OV-Chipkaart fares for city transportation. It works for busses, trams and subways. I personally love this app because it's updated quite often, regarding constructions and delays.

4. Bring a Debit Card

This is a life hack that also saved me a lot. I opened a bank account here and the bank just gave me a debit card. I usually prefer to use a credit card, so I thought it was really strange that I got a card with just one function. A day later I found out that the establishments here don't accept credit cards at all.

Some of the supermarkets here don't even cashiers anymore, just one supervisor that can help you if you're searching for something and the people that are buying something that checks the products out with a debit card.

I also found out that most establishments, like bars, restaurants and even the movie theatre, don't accept cash payments. They prefer debit payment being easier and better for the environment once less bills are printed.

5. Cooking or Eating Out?

Restaurants usually are pretty expensive here save from an odd one or other. The truth is, Dutch food isn't the greatest thing in the world and if you're staying more than a week in a place that you can cook, you can save a lot of money.

What people don't actually tell you is that the promotions in some supermarkets are just valid if you have the bonus card. In the beginning I didn't know that and I was still paying full price for products that were technically in a promotional price. I then found out that it's handed to the consumer a bonus card that you activate online and it gives you special prices on certain products. So every time I go shopping, I take my bonus card with me to get great deals.

6. Rent a Bike

If you want the whole Dutch experience and don't want to spend a lot of money with transportation, you can rent a bike. There are a lot places to rent for a day or two some bikes but my suggestion is to rent from the NS (yes, the train company) because it's safer and it's a bargain.

Bikes are the most used way of transportation here and I was amazed when I found out how many types of bikes there are. There are bikes for women so it's possible to bike with a dress or a skirt, there are bikes with baby or dog carriers, there are folding bikes, and the list goes on. There are special lanes for bikes, as well as traffic lights and parking all over the city.

There's just one thing that it's important to know is that driving a bike while drunk is a crime and you'll be arrested and you'll have to pay a fine. The police here are oftentimes in civilian clothes and patrol gets intense during night time.

7. Take a Free Tour Around the City

There are some services in the Hague that allows tourists to take a free walking or biking tour around the city. These tours can vary between 15km to 25km, depending on what you want to see. They show museums, parks, the beach and important buildings around the city. It usually takes the whole day, but it's conducted in a calm pace to everyone's comfort.

8. Using free Wi-Fi

There are some things in life that we can't live without and internet seems to be one of them. I don't remember the last time I had to use my 3G/4G in here. There's free Wi-Fi virtually everywhere from the trains and trams to the stores in the city center. It's not difficult to connect and all the public hotspots have proven to be reliable time and time again.

9. Buy a Museumkaart

The Museumkaart from the Hague is available online and it's a must have. It allows access to 19 of the 34 museums in the city, without any wait in lines. What I really like about this card is that it gives you a very hefty discount and it's valid for more than a week, so there's no need to go visiting all museums at once, you can stroll around the many galleries displayed.

10. Bring a Coat/Jacket

Turns out that even in the coastal city nobody is safe from the rain or the wind so be prepared to get wet and be blown away. I always go out with a jacket, independently if it's really hot outside and with not clouds in the sky because it will rain somewhere between you going out and you coming back. If by a miracle is doesn't rain, you will get a bit chilly from the gusts of wind that will come full force in your direction. Stay alert and always check any whether app you might have to see if there's any warning about the force of the wind or the intensity of the storms.

Bárbara Campos Diniz

Though I am often in the depths of misery,
the is still calmness, pure harmony and
music inside me.

Vincent van Gogh

Bárbara Campos Diniz

11. Buying (Legal) Drugs

Even though this topic is controversial, it's a fact that the consumption of pot and certain types of mushrooms is completely legal in the Netherlands. The Hague isn't a hub like Amsterdam in this perspective, but there are its fare shares of coffee shops. There are basically four things that it's a must know if you're going to experiment with these kind of drugs.

First of all, the minimum age to buy anything is 18 years (this is also held for alcoholic beverages). Second of all, there's a limit of grams that a person can carry, if you're busted by a cop you will get arrested and pay a hefty fine. Thirdly, it's not allowed to smoke in public places like the beach or the city center, you have two options, or you smoke in the café or at home. Last but not least, the closer you get to the city center, more expensive is the drug, so be aware of the prices and always compare.

12. Take a Look at the Haagse Markt

The Haagse Markt is located near the Station Holland Spoor. The market is open several times a week and it's the epitome of Dutch culture sent on one place. Over there you can buy fresh meat and fish, fruits, vegetables directly from the producers. Oftentimes it's cheaper to go grocery shopping there instead of the supermarkets. The market also sell second hand stuff. I really mean stuff because you can find the most bizarre things from locks without keys to leather bags and shoes. The Dutch can really sell anything!

13. To Beer or Not to Beer

If you come to the Hague and don't go to one of the many pubs the city has to offer, you haven't been in the Netherlands at all. There are two different types of bars in the Hague. There are ones that are a mixture of bar, restaurant and nightclub, and there are those really small bars that can actually be pubs.

The pubs here work a bit differently from other places because you have a selection up to 300 types of beer to choose from and it isn't an easy task. They offer blonde, red and dark beer, of all unimaginable flavors from different countries. It's really hard to decide so I usually go with whatever the barman suggests and I'm never disappointed.

14. Trying Dutch French Fries

Everyone in the world loves French fries, especially when they come in a burger combo. The thing is, the Dutch have reinvented this salty deliciousness. Here, there are snack bars that only sell French fries with dozens of different sauces to accompany them. In the Hague there are at least ten of those places up and down the city center streets.

The Dutch fries are amazing and not at all expensive. My personal favorite is call *fritjes speciaal* which literally means *special fries.* The reason they're special has to do with the fact that the sauce that comes with these fries is a mixture of mayonnaise, curry and diced onions.

15. Eating Marvelous Stroopwafels

When I first ate this wafel filled with caramel I thought I had found the most delicious thing on Earth. A few years later, and I still haven't found something that top it off. Stroopwafels, like the fries, are embedded in Dutch culture and it doesn't come to a surprise that there are a lot of places that sell them around the Hague.

There are basically two types of stroopwafels available, the cold one and the fresh one. The cold one can be found everywhere, from the drugstore to the supermarket and they're usually available in small, snack-like sizes to ones that fit in a desert plate. The fresh one is usually available in markets and they're served hot and to top all of that, these stroopwafels are three times bigger than the ones sold in stores.

16. Borrelhapjes

Borrelhapjes are basically the snacks consumed while enjoying a pint of beer with your friends or family. They usually are deep fried snacks, available in pubs, cafés and supermarkets. These *hapjes* are *croketen, bitterballen, frikandelen* and *kaassouflés.* Even though their names are a bit weird, they go along with basically ant beverage. The *croketen, bitterballen,* and *frikandelen* are made of minced and chopped meant while *the kaassouflés* have a cheese filling.

17. Eat Raw Fish

The Dutch have a peculiar cuisine at best. Even though I eat almost all their food, the one that got me attention was the *haaring*. Like other typical food mentioned above, the *haaring* also has a special place in the culture and is present in many places around the city, including the market. The *haaring* is a raw fish served with pickles, chopped onions and a slice of lemon. To be honest it doesn't look like much, but I assure you that at least trying a *haaring* is an experience that you will never forget.

18. Look Out for the Canals

Here in the Hague the canals aren't really used for tourism like in Amsterdam. They have a very special function in the annual festival *Jazz in de Gracht*. The free jazz festival happens around August and it's held in the picturesque canals in the Hague. The artists perform on boats and move along the canals until they find a spot and present. After a presentation the band move along and another one comes to fill its spot and so on. The atmosphere is fantastic to relax or to have a romantic date, soaking up the music and sipping some wine.

19. Enjoy the International Fireworks Festival

Every year, in Shceveningen, there's this amazing firework festival that attracts thousands of people. The festival offers up to two shows a night and it's a competition of teams from different countries that count on sound effects, colors and forms to create a spectacular show. It's always amazing to watch every teams outdoing each other while relaxing on the beach.

20. Eat as Much as You Can in the Hague Food Festival

This was my by far my favorite festival of all of them. The food festival showcases the best chefs and food and drink producers of the region. It's colorful and every stand holds a different surprise. The Hague is a very multicultural city, and the festival portrays how the food symbolizes their footprint in the city.

I was completely awed and I basically stuffed my face with everything that I could be my hands on. I tried food from many different restaurants and every single one of them were unique and delicious in their own way.

Bárbara Campos Diniz

The Dutch are very practical people.

Famke Janssen

Bárbara Campos Diniz

21. Visit the Museum van Kleef

This museum is one of the most beautiful hidden gems in the Hague. Even though it's quite popular with the residents, a lot of tourists never invent heard of this place. The Museum van Kleef is actually a functioning distillery, where people can discover the wonders of making a delicious alcoholic beverage. They also offer lunch and dinner in the picturesque environment for group and team tours.

22. Take a Gamble in the Holland Casino

The Holland Casino is by far the largest casino in the Hague, and the most profitable one. With an inviting and colorful atmosphere, the casino is a good place to try your luck and relax. It's also quite close to the beach, so after a winning, it's always good to have dinner in the many restaurants in the region. The minimum age to play any of the games available or even to enter the casino is 18 years.

23. Look up, Never Down

When walking around the Hague, try to appreciate the architecture surrounding you. The centuries of history the buildings hold upon them and the contrast between the old and the new. The Hague is a city in constant transformation, always looking into the future but never forgetting its past. As you walk down the city center you can feel the nostalgia and the modernization in the air, in the buildings and in the people. It's a wonder that such different styles come together so perfectly, as to compliment and complete one another much like puzzle pieces.

24. Take a Walk Through China Town

The Hague's China Town is the only one that I've actually been to so I won't compare it to the ones in London and New York. What I can say is that it's so beautiful how the oriental traces of China reverberates on the buildings, the food and the people but at the same time, it has hints of Dutch in them, much like a beautiful and successful mixture. China Town provides amazing food for low prices and invites everyone to take a peek in Chinese culture with festivals and the Chinese New Year's celebration.

25. Relax at the Grote Markt

Grote Markt is one of the best places in the city to grab a couple of beers with friends and family. The great thing about Grote Markt, besides the price of the beer, is that there are always concerts happening at least a couple of times there. The ambiance is fantastic and most concerts and festivals are free, as long as you sit down in many of the bars in the area and enjoy a cold beer with some barrelhapjes.

26. De Pip is the Place to Be

De Pip is always a place that draws attention to everyone in the Hague because it's a versatile space. It's not a club, or a bar, or a restaurant, but rather an old factory transformed in surreal and alternative events. This shows how an abandoned factory can still be of use to the citizens and tourists.

The events that are held at de Pip are numerous, going from vintage clothes sales to Halloween balls that are truly amazing and decadent. De Pip shows how Dutch people are all about finding new purposes to what's old and left aside. The events held at de Pip won't disappoint, especially if you've come prepared to party.

27. Take a Look at the Peace Palace

The Peace Palace is the most important juridical institution in the United Nations. Famously known to be the most celebrate center of International Law in the world, the Peace Palace is an important landmark in European and world History considering the many peace treaties and conventions that were and still are held in the building. The Palace is world of marvel and wonder to those interested in the field and is open to visitation a few weeks during summer holidays. The tour is always guided and can be scheduled online.

28. See the Sint Jacobskerk

This church in the city center is dated back to the 15th century and over the years has been in numerous reformations. Even though the protestant church may look like any other, it holds different functions such as art exhibitions, a café and a restaurant, concerts, choir presentations and, of course, mass. The church tower is one of the tallest towers in the Hague and it's open to the public to climb its 288 steps. The view from thee tower is beautiful but I wasn't able to have a very good panoramic view since there were some tall buildings blocking my way.

29. Go See a Musical

The Circustheater in Scheveningen is one of the most charismatic buildings I have even seen. To be honest it isn't much to look at, but the atmosphere is completely cozy and classy at the same time. Besides being accessible and close to the Holland Casino, the Circustheater is really good to spend some quality time together with the family. There are always Broadway musicals in theatres and tickets are available online.

30. Discover the Paard van Troje

The Paard van Troje is the biggest concert hall in the Hague. Besides having a very nice venue and acoustics, the staff is as friendly as they come. What I liked most about this place is that it's completely affordable and the agenda is very diverse. I went there several times to see different artists and orchestras and every time I stepped through those doors I felt I was in a different place every single time.

Bárbara Campos Diniz

A true artist perseveres… not matter what the critics say.

Dutch Proverb

Bárbara Campos Diniz

31. We'll Never Be Royals

The Paleis Noordeinde is the official residency of the Dutch Royal family, and where King Willem work as chief of State. The palace is one of the most well-known symbols of the Hague and is situated in the exact center of the city. Even though the Palace isn't open to the public, it's possible to stroll through the royal gardens and get close to the building. The gardens are as majestic as the Palace itself, allowing people to explore its various paths.

32. Let's Party!

There's a place in the city center called *de Plaats* which literally means 'the square'. This place is the major hub for clubbing in the Hague. However, the clubs are more a mixture of a bar, a restaurant with a dancing hall. When I stepped into one of those for my birthday celebration, I was taken aback because while there were a lot of clubs to choose from, all of them were pretty small compared to the ones that I'm used to. Nonetheless, I got a celebratory bottle of Champaign and discounts for me and my friends on all our drinks that night. The only thing that I can say is that going clubbing here has always been a very good experience to me.

33. Be Godzilla for One Day

One of the most well known parks in the Netherlands is the Madurodam. I love going there so I can feel like Godzilla for a day. The Madurodam is a gigantic miniature city park that portrays in the minimum details some Dutch monuments in a very organic way. You can take a stroll around the buildings and the monuments and the canals. One of my most remarkable memory is when I observed how the uneven canals in the Netherlands allowed boats to pass along them with an old technology. It's a bit hard to explain but, according to the level of water on one side of the gate, the other side of the gate (the one with the boat) will empty or add more water so both sides can level and the boat can get through.

34. Contemplate the Binnenhof

The Binnenhof is the heart of the Dutch government and where the most important political decisions were made throughout history. The building has been used by the Dutch Parliament since the 15th century and nowadays is the head-quarters of the Prime Minister of the Netherlands. It's possible to visit the Binnenhof with a guided tour of the grounds. The complex also counts on a very neogothic fountain right next to the building and an enormous lake, perfect for a stroll or a picnic on a warm summer afternoon.

35. Take a Look at the Ridderzaal

The Ridderzaal, or the Knight's Hall is actually a part of the Binnenhof but it's more special than any other part of the complex and it deserves its own tip. The Knight's Hall was built after the Binnenhof was purchased and put to use as the center of the Dutch Government. The Hall is where the Dutch Parliament and the Dutch King comes together in a celebratory speech on Prince's Day. To me, this traditional meeting is important to show how united the government really is and to show this union to the citizens. The Knight's Hall is open to the public through guided visitation and the splendor of the building and the royal throne are worth going for.

36. A Walk Through the Japanese Garden

The Japanese Garden is the heart of a park in the Hague. The garden is a marvel and worth having a good walk until you get there. The garden is really colorful and fragile, making it open to visitation 6 months in a year. The Japanese Garden is a place where someone can find true serenity and relax due to the harmony and balance of the trees, flowers, pond and vegetation.

37. Visit the Rose Garden

There's another park in the Hague, called the Westbrokpark, that is considered one of the most beautiful parks in the city. It was designed in the 1920s and since then, many people enjoy hot summer days relaxing with loved ones. The crown jewel of the park is the rose garden that is internationally know for its beauty and for its size. The garden has thousands upon thousands of rose bushes flowering between July and October. It's the perfect place to take a romantic walk.

38. Go to the Museum Gevangenpoort

The Gevangenpoort Museum is was actually the Prison Gate in the Hague for many centuries. The museum can only be visited with a guided tour that explains the torture process and what the cells were used to, among showing artifacts and some paintings. The worst part of the experience is hearing the 'ghost stories' that the guides tell during the tours and the ambiance doesn't really help with the slight chill that goes down your spine. The Prison Gate Museum isn't really popular among tourists but it's a must see if you're interested in a bit of Dutch history.

39. Mauritshuis, a Must See

The Mauritshuis is one of the most famous museums in the Netherlands and can be considered the crown jewel when it come to the Dutch painters of the Golden Age. The collection is not as large as the one in the Rijksmuseum in Amsterdam but it holds important pieces for Dutch and international art history. The exhibitions in the museum count with famous painting like The Bull by Potter, The Girl with the Pearl Earring by Vermeer and The Anatomy Lesson by Rambrandt. The museum offers a unique experience and tells the tales of the Dutch and Flemish artists that are admired around the world.

40. Visit the Hague Municipal Museum

 The Municipal Museum is less known than other museum but it doesn1t make it important to visit. The Municipal Museum has the largest Mondrian collection in the world, including his last work. Furthermore, the museum also aggregates the Museum of Contemporary Art and the Hague Museum for Photography, even though they're separate collections. From the modern architecture to the collections, this museum is a far cry from the historic museums in the Hague.

Bárbara Campos Diniz

Experience was my only teacher; I knew little of the modern art movement. When I first saw the works of the Impressionists, van Gogh, van Dongen, and Fauves, I admired it. But I had to seek the true way alone.

Piet Mondrian

Bárbara Campos Diniz

41. The Escher in het Paleis

There are two aspects that makes this museum famous and worth visiting. The first one of them is that the building where the museum is currently situated, was the Winter Palace for the Royal Family as well as the offices of the last queens until Queen Beatrix moved everything to Paleis Noordeinde. There's a past of the building dedicated to the brief history of the Royal Family in the place.

The second reason is the man who gave the museum its name. Escher's international recognition for his optical illusion drawings and paintings awarded his works of art to be displayed in a special museum dedicated just for him. However, in 2015 it was revealed that the art in the museum wasn't the original Eschers but rather a printed version of them. Until this day it's not certain if they changed the replicas for the real deal or not, but it's worth to check it out.

42. Shop Till You Drop

There are two places in the Hague that can be compared to the Los Angeles' Rodeo Drive or even the Champs Elysée in Paris and they are the Bijenkorf and De Passage. The Bijenkorf is the second oldest department store in the Hague. Nowadays its space is dedicated to exclusive and exceptionally expensive brands. The main focus of the Bijenkorf is focused on giving an inspiring and unique experience to its consumers.

De Passage is just as exclusive as the Bijenkorf even though the stores are a bit more accessible to the general public with the presence of restaurants and cafés. If you're feeling fancy and wants to do a bit of shopping, this is your way to go.

43. Finding Vintage Shops

There's something that I've always admired in Dutch culture that just now reached the rest of the world, vintage clothes. The Dutch don't like wasting anything so instead of throwing away a perfectly good shirt just because you got bored, they sell it to vintage shops. In the Hague there are a lot of vintage shops scattered around the city. All of them offer good products with an outstanding quality that are recycled and put in the window again. I found the most exquisite pieces for my wardrobe that I bought for pennies while the modern version usually costs a fortune. Vintage shopping is fun, it's environmentally friendly and a great way to find unique and quirky pieces.

44. Hiking in the Meijendel Park

The best place to hike in the Hague is the Maijendel Natural Reserve. I stubbled across this place when I was walking around Scheveningen on a sunny day. The Meijendel Reserve is the largest natural reserve in Zuid-Holland and it's characterized by its dunes and lakes. The landscape is unique and very beautiful. There are a lot of hiking routes that are really different from each other and takes us to there amazing places. I know that hiking may not be conventional to a lot of tourists, but the park won't disappoint you.

45. Having a Great Day in Scheveningen

There's absolutely nothing more enjoyable than spending the day at the beach during the summer holidays. Scheveningen seems like a small town within the city. It can just chilling on the sand, or walking up and down the beachfront, Scheveningen offers a lot of activities, festivals and relaxing time. My favorite part of the beach is the pier, where you can see the sea and its dark blue water, and an eventual whale on the horizon.

46. Visiting the Museum Beelden aan Zee

This museum is located on a resort near the beach and it's completely accessible to all public. The museum itself is hidden in the dunes making it isolated from the busy and noisy world. The inside of the museum is relaxing and quite, a place perfect to gather your thoughts and take a break from everything. The outside of the museum is everchanging. While in the summer it's lovely to walk across the picture centers and the patios and drink a cool and refreshing drink, during the winter, the atmosphere is serene when the beach is left to take its natural course. It's mesmerizing to watch.

47. Having a Drink at the Haagse Toren

The Haagse Toren is one of the tallest building in the city with one of the most spectacular views I have ever see. The past floor of the building is a sky bar and restaurant with an amazing assortment of cocktails and food. There are a lot of great parties that happens in the tower that are very popular among college students. The atmosphere is quite different from the party nights to regular nights because while the place can be crazy and wild, it can also be serene and romantic.

48. Looking at a City in a Canvas

There's one place in the Hague that I had one of my memorable experiences during my stay in the city . It was in the Panorama Mesdag, the largest circular canvas in the world. This canvas imitates Scheveningen in the end of the 19th century and it seems so real that you start to believe that painting is the real deal. Besides being an unique monument, the Panorama features the sea and the boats, the small village of Scheveningen and the sand dunes so characteristic of the region.

49. Celebrate 5 Mei

The celebration of May 5th is one of the most important traditions in Dutch history. The date celebrates Liberation day, the day the Netherlands was free from the Nazis after World War II. The celebration counts with military parades and free concerts around the city. It's very beautiful to see how people come together to celebrate freedom and to remember those who lost their lives protecting their country.

50. Happy Birthday to the King!

King's Day is my favorite Dutch celebration among all of them. The birthday of the king seems to be the birthday of all. Huge music festivals happens in the Hague during the celebratory day and people go absolutely crazy. It's customary to everyone to dress in orange or with the colors with the flag. The Dutch go all out with wigs, paints, funny costumes and lots of beer. Besides the carnival, it's customary for the Royal Family to take a walk around the city during the King's celebratory day so people can wish him a happy birthday. The people also have the tradition to sell the stuff they don't need anymore, turning the streets of the Hague in an enormous flea market. I absolutely adored being here and celebrate King's Day in the Netherlands.

Bárbara Campos Diniz

> TOURIST

GREATER THAN A TOURIST

Visit GreaterThanATourist.com
http://GreaterThanATourist.com

Sign up for the Greater Than a Tourist
Newsletter
http://eepurl.com/cxspyf

Follow us on Facebook:
https://www.facebook.com/GreaterThanATourist

Follow us on Pinterest:
http://pinterest.com/GreaterThanATourist

Follow us on Instagram:
http://Instagram.com/GreaterThanATourist

Bárbara Campos Diniz

> TOURIST

GREATER THAN A TOURIST

Please leave your honest review of this book on Amazon and Goodreads. Thank you.

We appreciate your positive and negative feedback as we try to provide tourist guidance in their next trip from a local.

> TOURIST

GREATER THAN A TOURIST

You can find Greater Than a Tourist books on Amazon.

Bárbara Campos Diniz

> TOURIST

GREATER THAN A TOURIST

WHERE WILL YOU TRAVEL TO NEXT?

Bárbara Campos Diniz

> TOURIST

GREATER THAN A TOURIST

Our Story

Traveling is a passion of this series creator. She studied abroad in college, and for their honeymoon Lisa and her husband toured Europe. During her travels to Malta, an older man tried to give her some advice based on his own experience living on the island since he was a young boy. She thought he was just trying to sell her something. When traveling to some places she was wary to talk to locals because she was afraid that they weren't being genuine. She created this book series to give you as a tourist an inside view on the place you are exploring and the ability to learn what locals would like to tell tourist.   A topic that they are very passionate about.

Bárbara Campos Diniz

> TOURIST

GREATER THAN A TOURIST

Notes